# Praise for Tough Shit

"Arianne MacBean's journal brings attention to an often-overlooked emotion. Anger can keep us mired in the past or it can become a catalyst for creative action. Women have carried injustice in their bodies for centuries, but anger turned into resolve becomes the clear-eyed wisdom we need to move forward today."

   - Elinor Dickson, Ph.D., author of *Dancing at the Still Point* and co-author with Marion Woodman of *Dancing in the Flames: The Dark Goddess in the Transformation of Consciousness*

As a divorce coach who helps women leave toxic, abusive marriages, I am *so* here for this journal. "My clients' rage is righteous and powerful—yet patriarchy tells them it's wrong. Part of my work is helping them reclaim anger as fuel for growth and empowerment. This journal is an invaluable tool."

   - Kate Anthony, host of *The Divorce Survival Guide Podcast* and author of *The D Word – making the ultimate decision about your marriage*

I have often searched for texts that reflected my belief in the inevitability, significance, and power of women's anger. There are so many books -- across academic psychology, self-help, and Buddhism -- that decry anger as negative, harmful, and unsightly. Or that suggest that women find peace by transcending her indignation. Amidst these are some authors who reassure me, who speak not only from their own embodied experience but from that of so many other women. Pick up the work of Lynne Thompson, Amanda Montei, Sandra Cisneros, Soraya Chemaly, Carolee Schneemann, or Adrienne Rich. Read Arianne MacBean: she is in excellent company!

   - Mady Schutzman, Ph.D., author of *The Real Thing: Performance, Hysteria, and Advertising* and *Radical Doubt*.

"This anger journal feels like the sweetest gift, a safe outlet when you need it the most."

   - Satya Doyle Byock, author of *Quarterlife* and director of The Salome Institute of Jungian Studies

Arianne MacBean effectively uses her separate realms of deep experience and training as a dance educator and marriage counselor to create a book that reminds us of the power and potency of mind-body connectivity and somatic neurology in influencing and regulating our emotional states.

- Jonathan R. Weinstein, MD, PhD Professor, Neurology University of Washington, Seattle, WA

Brava to Arianne MacBean for creating this brave, bold and much-needed self-reflection journal! *Tough Shit* gives women the space to be raw, real, and unapologetic. Inside, you'll find prompts and practices to help you express your anger, face your fears, move through sadness, and sit with hurt — all aimed at reconnecting you with your true self. *Tough Shit* is your place to rage, release, and reclaim your power. It is time.

- Tabby Biddle, bestselling author of *Find Your Voice: A Woman's Call to Action*

We each find our path to healing in different ways. This journal gives voice to emotions that are often dismissed and encourages honest self-inquiry. A powerful resource for those ready to turn toward their feelings and rise stronger on the other side.

- Michelle Dozois, fitness and wellness expert, co-founder breakthruYOU

For every big feeling, a way through. Anti-oppressive, accessible, and truly transformative—this is a resource we all need. *Tough Shit* reframes anger, fear, sadness, and hurt as pathways to truth, combining somatic practices and writing prompts to guide readers toward embodiment and processing.

- Anne Kinsey, author of *Find Your Fucking Fire* and *Mosaic Hearts*

*Tough Shit*. Arianne MacBean's no-nonsense normalization of human emotions combined with practical writing prompts and somatic exercises, guides the reader through a full body experience of honoring feelings society has long encouraged us to feel ashamed of, channeling anger and hurt into self-discovery and healing.

- Laura M. Alie, PsyD, Assistant Director, High Acuity Programs, University Health Services UC Berkeley

# Tough Shit

Arianne MacBean

TEHOM CENTER

Tehom Center Publishing is a 501(c)3 nonprofit publishing feminist and queer authors, with a commitment to elevate BIPOC writers. Its face and voice is Rev. Dr. Angela Yarber.

Paperback ISBN: 978-1-966655-48-0

Ebook ISBN: 978-1-966655-49-7

*This book is dedicated to all the angry women out there. You know who you are.*

*I snarl in solidarity with you!*

*Anger is an assertion of rights and worth. It is communication, equality, and knowledge. It is intimacy, acceptance, fearlessness, embodiment, revolt, and reconciliation. Anger is memory and rage. It is rational thought and irrational pain. Anger is freedom, independence, expansiveness, and entitlement. It is justice, passion, clarity, and motivation. Anger is instrumental, thoughtful, complicated, and resolved. In anger, whether you like it or not, there is truth.*

SORAYA CHEMALY

# Acknowledgments

Forever and always, I hold deep love for my family, Will, Lily, and Claire who remind me to never stop cultivating my truest self. Big thanks goes out to my editor Ahnie Litecky for her enthusiasm and eagle eye. This book would not exist without the support of my spiritual sister and friend for life, Angelina Schneider who has encouraged me at every step to feel, express, and create. Lastly, I extend heartful gratitude to my brave and perfectly imperfect clients who inspired this journal and its celebration of feelings as a road map toward self-knowledge. It's one of my life's greatest honors to walk the path with you.

# Introduction

As a marriage and family therapist, I have found that many of my women clients come to counseling believing anger is a shameful feeling that must be obliterated. They demonize and label anger as problematic, crazy, or worse, stupid. They try to affirm their way out of this feeling but find themselves returning to it over and over again. Affirmations can be nice, but we need to feel our feelings, not talk ourselves out of them. Sometimes shitty things are just shitty, and it is not helpful or appropriate to strong-arm them into being positive life lessons. If I never see another self-improvement journal that suggests taking a walk in the sunshine, putting on comfy slippers, or baking a batch of cookies, it will be too soon. Those directives alone inspire rage! To learn from big divisive feelings, we must let them exist and listen to them, not fake-affirm them into an advertisement for crescent rolls. By reframing our relationship with anger as a potent smoke signal for the vital fire within, we can stoke the flames of transformation in ourselves and our world.

Expressing and tuning into our big emotions is tricky. We shouldn't yell at our children, partners, colleagues, or parents, but we have real aggravation that needs to be honored. We are not supposed to flip off a reckless driver or put our hand in the face of an aggressive neighbor, but we feel fear course through our body. We feel silly crying in front of our friends or embarrassed when we spontaneously sob while watching the toilet paper commercial on TV, but we carry deep sorrow that aches to be released. The thing is, anger, fear, sadness, and hurt are important signals pointing us toward our root pain, a core part of who we are and how we experience our world. These big feelings are the map of our road of reactivity, which, if we follow mindfully, we can learn from and use to make important shifts toward more fulfilling lives.

# How This Journal Works

The pages within this interactive journal are a safe place for all your shit. Here, you have full permission to feel the depth of your contempt, dread, despair, and heartache. However, it doesn't end there. While you move through these feelings, you are also mapping their connectivity to locate a core pain point at the center of all the so-called "negative" emotions. At this locus, you are given the space to implement your new self-knowledge toward actionable change. With compassion and realness, *Tough Shit.* provides an outlet for the crap no one wants to hear (except your therapist) but that your own soul demands to understand. Most importantly, you gain tools to understand why you feel the way you feel and how to translate this knowledge into real-life transformation.

Whether you have recently started to experience big heavy feelings or have been carrying them around for years, this journal provides the freedom to express your genuineness. Start with anger, the easily accessible, high-intensity moment when you blow up or break down. Then, progressively traverse through the moderately intense emotions of fear and sadness, because underneath anger there are always more vulnerable feelings. Hurt is the most defenseless of emotions, so we call it your core pain point. Here, we get as close to our most defenseless part by being honest about what the activation is truly about—usually some part of yourself about which you feel deeply insecure. Finally, you integrate the connective insight you have gained by following your road of reactivity to true self, where you envision how you can actively engage your new self-knowledge in your day-to-day life.

Practice the somatic exercise as you go, and use the journal prompts to write freely, in a stream of consciousness, with no judgment or editing. Try to keep your pen moving on the paper nonstop and, if you get stuck, just repeat the last word you wrote until you un-stick yourself and then keep writing. Work your way through the journal by writing on any prompts that call to you from each section:

- Section I: Anger
- Section II: Fear
- Section III: Sadness
- Section IV: Hurt

After completing the first four sections, read backward from Hurt to Anger to gain insight into how your vulnerable self relates to your triggered self, tracking your road of reactivity. Conclude by writing on the prompts and doing the somatic exercises in:

- Section V: True Self.

# The Road of Reactivity

Feeling and expressing your difficult emotions is important for its own benefits, such as honoring your authenticity, actively working against repression, and the release of toxic energy. Anger and fear are signals that something feels defenseless in you. That's why this journal prompts you to start with your activated and triggered self (BIG feelings) and eases you toward your vulnerable self (smaller feelings). After you progress through the first four stages, you will discover the part of you that feels the most exposed, or at risk. When you acknowledge the small but essential part of yourself that feels susceptible to harm, your true self can hold it with compassion. It is from a compassionate place that we feel empathy towards ourselves and others. By working through this journal consciously and somatically, not only are you expressing your feelings and uncovering why you react the way you do, but you also ultimately utilize this self-knowledge toward existing in an *embodied self*. And this, fellow feelers, is the golden egg.

## THE ROAD OF REACTIVITY
### FEELING DIFFICULT EMOTIONS

# What is an Embodied Self and Why Would I Want One?

An embodied self is the experience of being fundamentally connected to your physical body. You don't have to be a guru to have an embodied self. You just need to slow down for a few minutes and focus on whatever sensations are present—good, bad, or nothing at all. Again, the aim here is not to eliminate our sensations but to approach them as helpful information. The experience of an embodied self encompasses awareness of your interoception, the signals you receive about the state of your body. If you are connected to your body, to its growing edges and resources, you are engaging your real capacity as a human being. An embodied self is a way of never being separated from your physical form but instead *integrating with it*. And why would you want to do that? Because your body is the only thing that is truly yours. It is the vessel that houses YOU. It holds a wealth of power because you can *move it* and *feel it*. The embodied YOU holds a deep sense of being present in the here and now and actively interacts with the world through these sensations. Basically, embodiment is your superpower.

# Somatic Pop-Ups

Throughout this journal there are simple body-based exercises that you can do before, during, or after a writing session. These pop-up experiences support attunement with the body, release of emotions, and activation of self-care. At the end of each exercise, you are reminded to "Note how you feel." This is an important moment, as it involves sending your focus inward, into your interior landscape, to sense the minute shifts or adjustments that may (or may not) have occurred in the somatic practice: Remember, it's all helpful information. Current research indicates that somatic movement, executed consciously while focusing on internal experience, can reduce stress, help one self-regulate, and improve general wellness. Performing somatic exercises while processing difficult emotions can facilitate an embodied sense of inner change. Feeling, in your body, the power of emotional sensations can bring relief, even joy. Use the somatic pop-ups as you progress through the journal. Return to exercises that feel particularly helpful to you, and fine-tune or adjust the exercises to your specific needs. Everybody and every body is unique. The somatic pop-ups are included here as a reminder that being close to yourself is life's magic elixir. It's where real insight and change occurs.

# What This Journal is NOT

Responding to the prompts and doing the exercises here is *not* a replacement for real, human-to-human therapy. Research shows that the relational quality of therapy is the most important aspect of the healing process, where your feelings and thoughts can be held by another person, mirrored back to you and, if necessary, reframed toward more productive relationships with self and others. This journal is best used in tandem with counseling that supports working deeply and tenderly with the way pain points relate to behaviors. The work in this journal can support the creation of a therapeutic alliance with a trained professional who you trust. Working with a therapist as you engage with your rising emotional awareness can help you develop ways to catch yourself before you are triggered and also strengthen emotional resiliency. And lastly, if you are diagnosed with a mental health disorder, always consult with your doctor to make sure this kind of interactive journal is helpful for your healing journey.

# Why This Journal Helps

In therapy with my clients, I have witnessed the powerful positive change that comes from tuning into, not shutting down, the big, blustering (but never bad) emotions that we all experience. This journal exists because of the real-life needs of my clients for more than just a weekly 50-minute therapy session to feel, express, and get closer to their big feelings and hard-to-access emotions. My clients needed (and deserved!) private safe space to process how their road of reactivity influences the ways they think, feel, and behave. Through using these writing prompts and somatic techniques, I have witnessed relief, ease, laughter, and even delight in my clients. So, get angry! Feel your feelings, acknowledge them, honor them! Get closer to your true self and let the realness of your humanness be your greatest power for actionable growth.

# Section 1: Anger

## Greetings Fellow Raging Maniac!

Anger is a normal human emotion. Everybody feels it. Anger is a sign that we have been threatened and feel unsafe and it is a way our body tries to protect us from harm. Often, anger points us toward an unmet need, a boundary crossing, or an obstacle keeping us from being who we truly are or living the way we want to live. Additionally, our anger at someone or something can actually be misattributed dismay that we feel about ourselves. This is why it is so important to slow down and honor anger, as it is a valuable emotion trying to keep us authentic. However, what we do when anger arises can lead us astray from our core self. Few of us are taught how to productively feel and express anger, and other than the therapy office, there are few places where anger is accepted.

This section of the journal is where you can express your burning fury in a safe and healthy way. Anger is an emotion we have been conditioned to repress for fear of being labeled disruptive, hysterical, difficult, or out of control. When locked away, anger can turn into resentment, which can become a lifelong hobby. Don't let anger turn toxic and take over your existence! It is a hint that something is not OK. It's true that we cannot bash people's brains out, scream obscenities, or throw ourselves on the floor, but that does not mean we have to obliterate or stuff down our indignation. In fact, it's necessary and healthy to process wild wrath, toxic resentment, and blind fury because we have reasons to feel that way! We must accept the feelings to understand them.

Your anger is welcome here.

I am losing my shit like a normal human being.

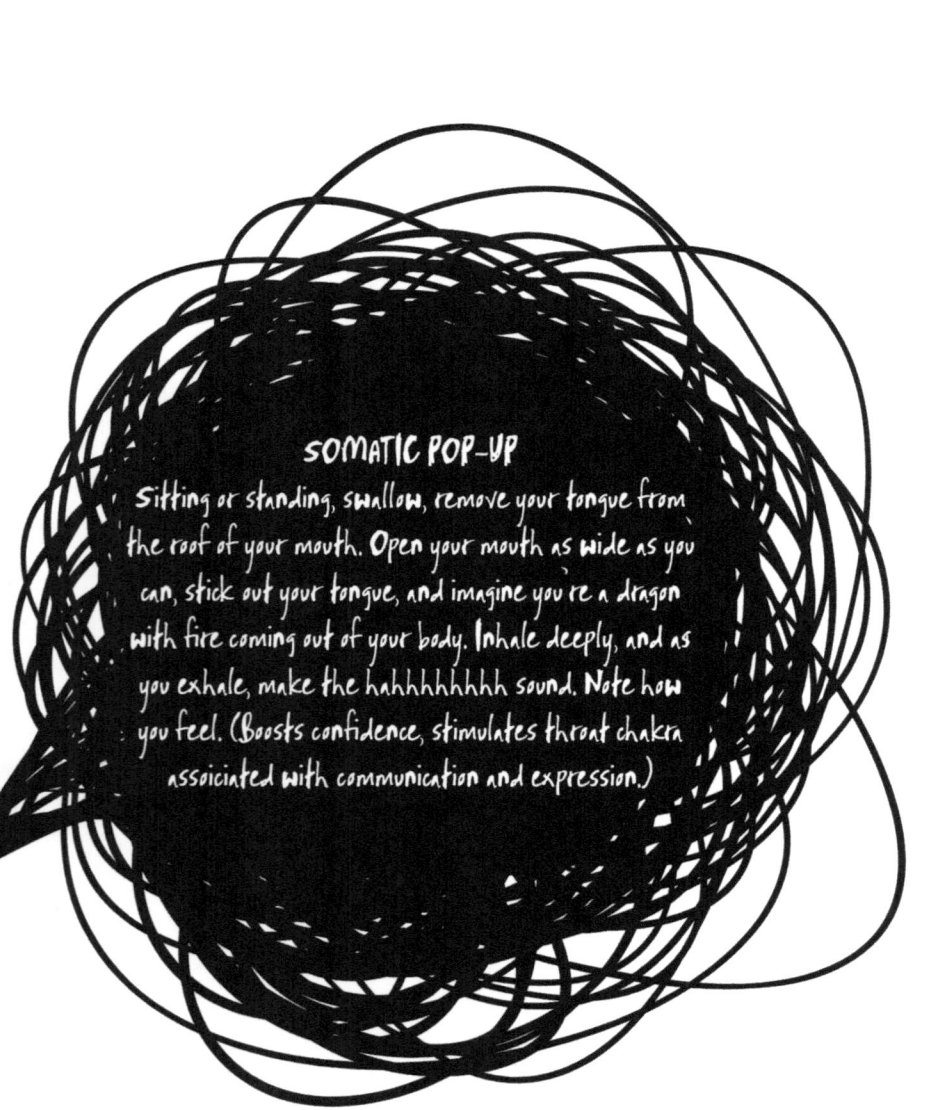

### SOMATIC POP-UP

Sitting or standing, swallow, remove your tongue from the roof of your mouth. Open your mouth as wide as you can, stick out your tongue, and imagine you're a dragon with fire coming out of your body. Inhale deeply, and as you exhale, make the hahhhhhhhh sound. Note how you feel. (Boosts confidence, stimulates throat chakra assoiciated with communication and expression.)

My internal fire is hot shit.

I am livid right now and it's f*cking important.

My indignation is The Shit.

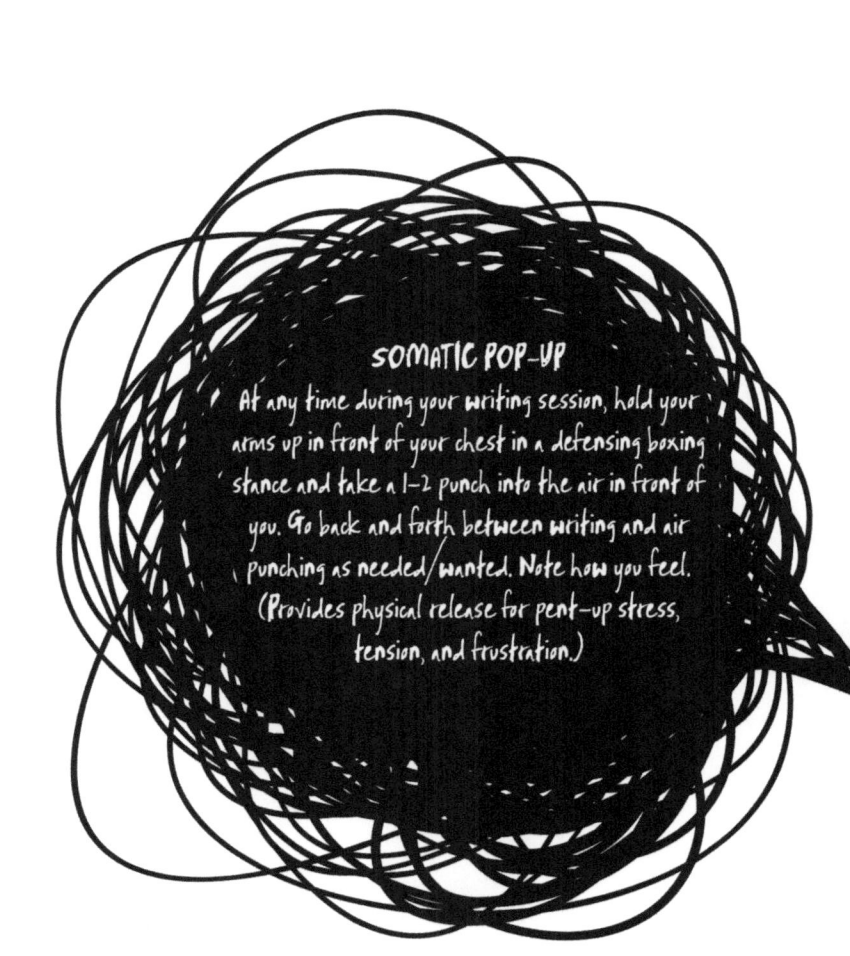

**SOMATIC POP-UP**
At any time during your writing session, hold your arms up in front of your chest in a defensing boxing stance and take a 1–2 punch into the air in front of you. Go back and forth between writing and air punching as needed/wanted. Note how you feel. (Provides physical release for pent-up stress, tension, and frustration.)

I do not feel shitty about my righteous outrage.

My contempt is real. I am not shitting you.

SOMATIC POP-UP

Sitting or standing, stomp your feet on the ground heavily for 10 seconds. Left, right, left, right. Note how you feel. (Provides a sense of grounding by stimulating the proprioceptors in your feet.)

Giving a shit is absolutely acceptable.

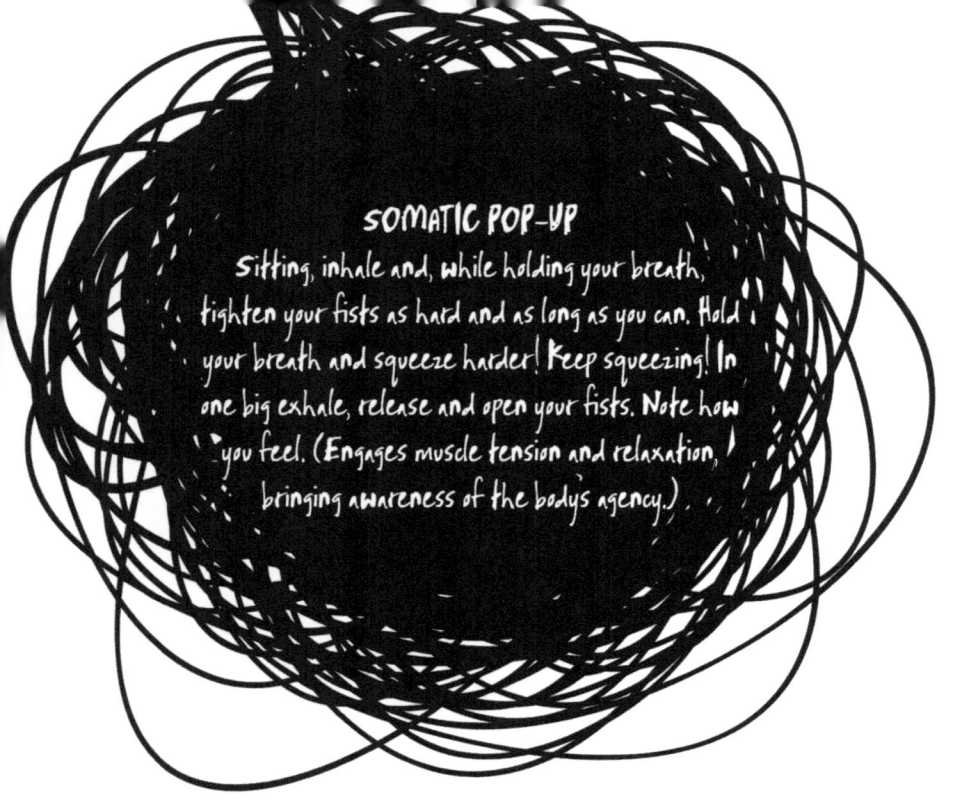

### SOMATIC POP-UP
Sitting, inhale and, while holding your breath, tighten your fists as hard and as long as you can. Hold your breath and squeeze harder! Keep squeezing! In one big exhale, release and open your fists. Note how you feel. (Engages muscle tension and relaxation, bringing awareness of the body's agency.)

My anger is here because it needs to be seen, heard, and felt.

Shit! All my triggers are pulled and there might be more.

I honor the breadth and depth of my fury.

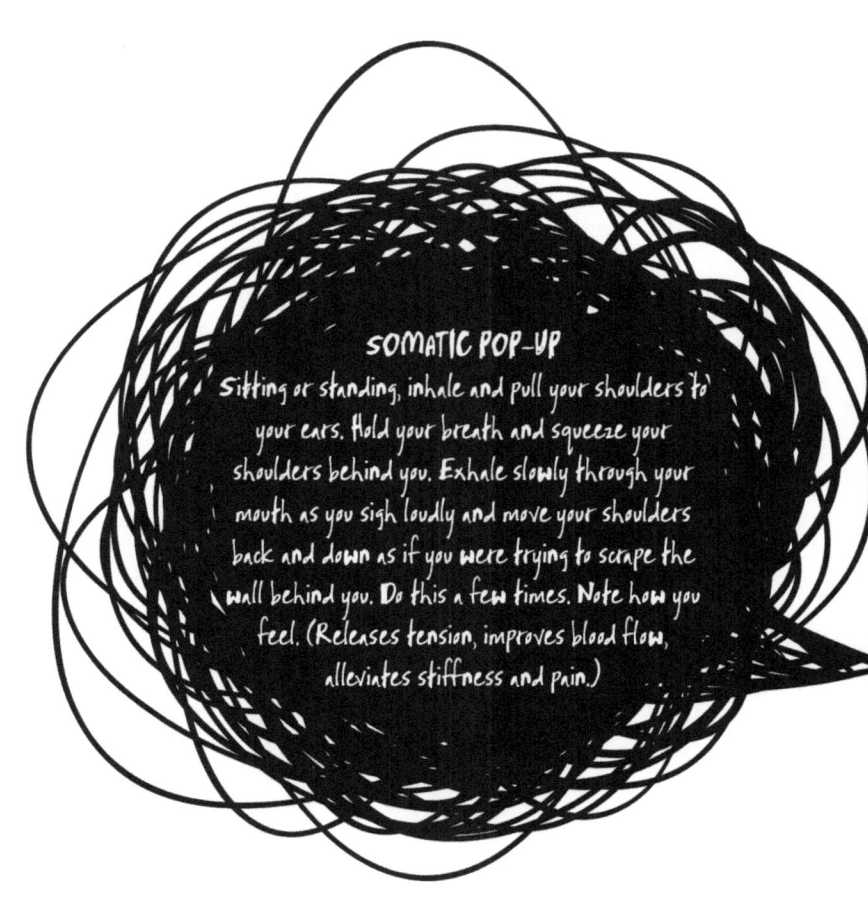

**SOMATIC POP-UP**

Sitting or standing, inhale and pull your shoulders to your ears. Hold your breath and squeeze your shoulders behind you. Exhale slowly through your mouth as you sigh loudly and move your shoulders back and down as if you were trying to scrape the wall behind you. Do this a few times. Note how you feel. (Releases tension, improves blood flow, alleviates stiffness and pain.)

I am f*cking pissed and that's the way shit goes sometimes.

I know that my vitriol is not unfounded.

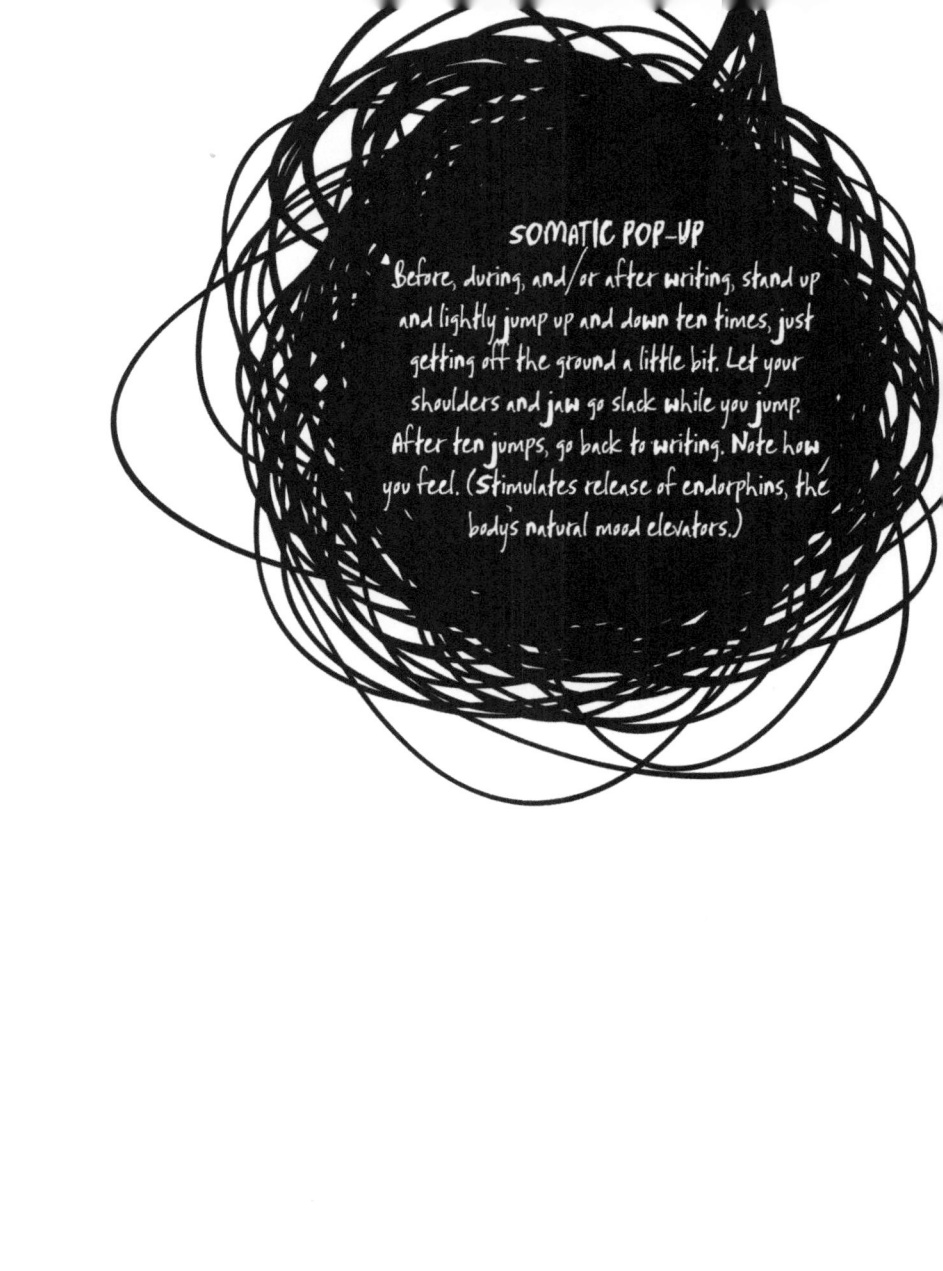

SOMATIC POP-UP
Before, during, and/or after writing, stand up and lightly jump up and down ten times, just getting off the ground a little bit. Let your shoulders and jaw go slack while you jump. After ten jumps, go back to writing. Note how you feel. (Stimulates release of endorphins, the body's natural mood elevators.)

I'm gonna shoot the shit out of how irate I feel

on this whole f*cking page.

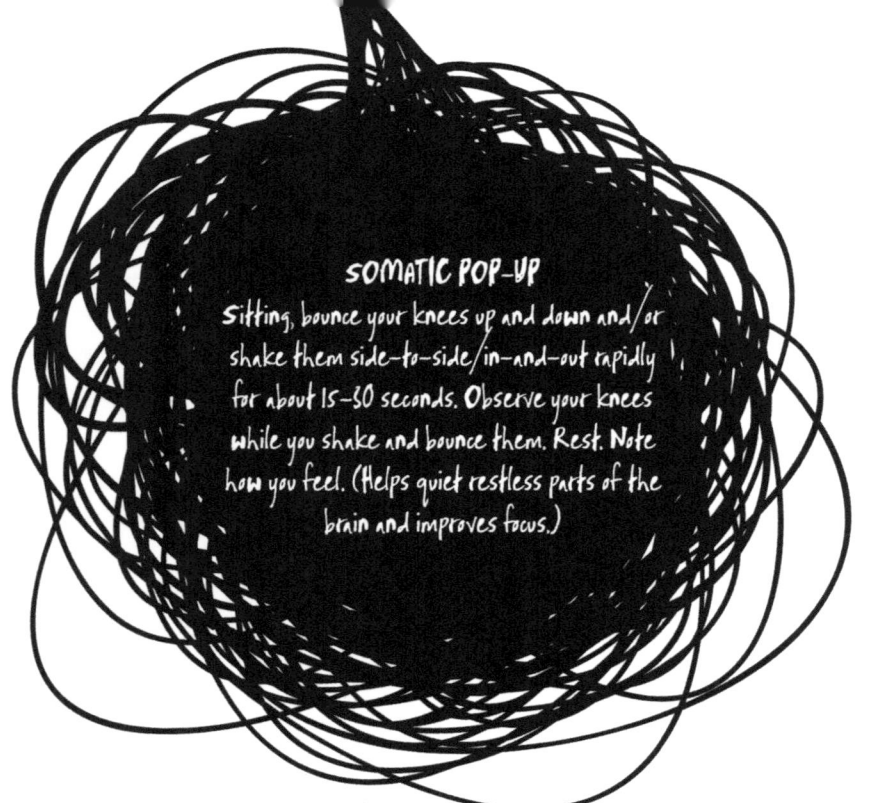

### SOMATIC POP-UP

Sitting, bounce your knees up and down and/or shake them side-to-side/in-and-out rapidly for about 15-30 seconds. Observe your knees while you shake and bounce them. Rest. Note how you feel. (Helps quiet restless parts of the brain and improves focus.)

How 'bout I trade your Live Laugh Love

for Fuck You Asshole.

I feel angry.

Crumple this page & throw it. Yep. Tear this page out of the book, squeeze it as tight as you can in your hand for a few seconds, then take a big inhale and on the exhale, hurl the ball of paper as hard as you can into a corner of your room. You may even want to add sound, like a deep guttural, "Ho!" while you hurl it. Note how it feels.

# Section 2: Fear

## Salutations Fellow Scaredy Cat!

You know fear. It's that tingling feeling, like tiny electric sparks firing up your nervous system. Sometimes it can make you feel hot, or cold, or hot and cold at the same time. Sometimes you can feel fear shoot into your brain and light it up like fireworks. Fear is important to notice because it connects us with our survival instincts, but we often avoid the feeling because, quite frankly, it's super uncomfortable. When fear hits, it hits hard, and so we clamp it down and tell ourselves, "Get over it. Don't be a wimp." The quick leap from terror to diminishment happens in the blink of an eye and before you know it, fear has been compartmentalized in the far reaches of your brain and body. And there it lives. Imagine living in the state of fear all the time, never being able to bring the stress cycle down to safety and reset—that is how many women live. No longer. This section of the journal is where you exalt in all your prickly panic and get to return to your secure self.

Every day, we face macro- and microaggressions that we must absorb and manage. Why should our alarm be dulled when it is one of the most common and natural of human experiences? One thing I hear regularly in therapy is clients expressing a sense of guilt or wickedness when they feel provoked by life's idiosyncrasies. When did we decide all interactions should be pleasurable? That is just one big fat fantasy. Life is fucking scary! In these next pages, release your horror.

Your fear is welcome here.

I honor the shitstorm of my panic.

## SOMATIC POP-UP

Before you begin writing, press your pen onto this page of the journal. Focus on it and hold it there, pressing as hard as you can for as long as you want/can. Release and write! Note how you feel. (The tactile sensation of pressing promotes focus and clarity; releasing allows feelings to flow.)

My profound concern is warranted.

I revel in the curdling stench of my crap-induced terror.

I trust that my trepidation for bullshit is legitimate.

## SOMATIC POP-UP

Sitting or standing, reach both arms above your head and take a deep breath in. With an open-mouthed exhale, release your upper body down over your thighs (head swinging down too) while swinging your arms down and back. Repeat that 3-5 times. Note how you feel. (Rhythmic full body swinging calms the nervous system, reducing stress.)

My anxiety alarm is ringing off the hook.

I will not cancel my shitty worry.

## SOMATIC POP-UP

Stand with your feet hip distance apart with your hands on your hips, looking straight ahead for 1 minute. Just stand there, or, if it feels good to do so, rhythmically bounce/tap your heels into the ground by lifting your heels off the ground and then dropping them down. Note how you feel. (Power posing directs the brain toward confidence, bouncing/tapping heels stimulates the nervous system, releasing tension.)

I am not shitting myself about the depth of my abject terror.

## SOMATIC POP-UP

Sitting or standing, take a deep breath in and on the exhale, flutter your lips. Do this a few times. Note how you feel. (Lip trill releases facial muscles, improves breath control, and regulates voice.)

There is jack shit that does not freak me out right now and I need to own it.

Shit is happening and it's f*cking distressing.

I affirm the nightmare of this continuous crap.

My phobia of being tossed in shit is genuine.

My definition of horror is held in high esteem.

## SOMATIC POP-UP

Sitting or standing, place your palms at the base of the back of your head and release your chin to your chest. Let your hands gently press your head downward while allowing your elbows to fall forward and down. Stay like this for a few breaths. Note how you feel. (Releases neck muscles, changes blood flow to head, allows for the release of negative feelings.)

I do not have my shit together, and for the moment, that's ok.

I am so f*cking frightened right now.

**SOMATIC POP-UP**

Place the palms of your hands on your chest and gently pat your chest right, left, right, left, back and forth for a few moments. Note how you feel. (Tapping boosts mood and reduces emotional distress.)

I feel scared.

This page is your shield. Rip it out of the book and hold it out in front of you, like a protective safeguard. Hold it out with strong straight arms for 10 seconds. Imagine the shield as an extension of your body. Breathe easily and mindfully as you sense whatever comes up. Note how it feels.

# Section 3: Sadness

## Hello Fellow Sad Sack!

Time and time again in my therapy office, I work with clients to recognize and allow sadness into their experience. Perhaps it is because so many of us were told "Don't cry" that we have unconsciously labeled sadness as flawed or weak. There is often great discomfort when feelings of sadness wash over us, and we instinctively try to eradicate the distress. Sometimes we attempt to return to equilibrium by distracting ourselves with social media, reaching for the quick fix of the vape pen, or simply by reverting to old dysfunctional coping mechanisms. Many of us did not have caregivers who were able to tolerate our sadness because they never learned how to be OK with discomfort either. But I see sadness as a gracious space, not an obstacle to overcome, and certainly not a feeling to avoid. When we permit sadness to enter our body, mind, and spirit, we welcome the true imperfection of humanness. When we concede to the sensation of sadness, we begin to accept our small child parts that were never tended to. Here, we become the caregivers of our true selves.

This section of the journal is where you acknowledge your despondency and give it a voice. Here, you get to be weak and shaky, brittle and inadequate. Let your unguarded timidity rear its fainthearted head. There is no element of melancholy, longing, or ache that is off-limits. Let your twinges twinge and your throbbing throb. Sadness is an energetic feeling. It can flow and transform. Let it.

Your sadness is welcome here.

My disappointment is real.

I accept this shit-test as I mourn it.

## SOMATIC POP-UP

**S**queeze every muscle in your face as tight as you can. Tighter! Hold the squeeze for as long as you can and then release in one fell swoop. **N**ote how you feel. (This is a mini massage for your facial muscles, releasing built-up tension.)

It's normal to feel sad when dumb shit happens.

Shit has hit the fan, and it is reasonable to release my flooding grief.

### SOMATIC POP-UP

Sitting or standing, place your hands on opposite shoulders, folding your arms across your chest. Just breathe naturally for a bit in this posture. Note how you feel. (Hugging yourself releases oxytocin, calming the nervous system.)

I'm

allowing

this

desolation

to

permeate

my

soul.

## SOMATIC POP-UP

Sitting or standing, place your right hand on your belly and your left hand on your heart. For ten deep slow breaths, focus on the contact between your hands and your body. Feel the pressure of that tactile connection and the rise and fall of your belly and chest that occur while you breathe. Note how you feel. (Provides tactile stimulation and release of calming hormones, activates relaxation through diaphragmatic breathing.)

The dejection in my shit-stained heart deserves to be revered.

I choose to exult in my misery.

Devastation is coursing through my body.

## SOMATIC POP-UP

Sitting or standing, clap your hands once hard and start rubbing them together. Keep rubbing for as long as you can, generating a little heat. When you notice the temperature rise between your hands, pause and hold your palms over you face, fingertips resting on your eyebrows and the base of your palms just below the cheeks. Note how you feel. (Friction from rubbing creates warmth and soothing; touching your face stimulates pressure points and provides a sense of self-comfort.)

I

am

so

f*cking

sad.

## SOMATIC POP-UP

Sitting, drop your head to rest on your knees. Use a pillow if necessary, so that you can completely rest your head and torso. Let your arms dangle down toward the floor. Stay there for a few moments. Note how you feel. (Increases blood flow to the brain, enhances relaxation.)

Every single cell inside me is full of sorrow.

I am allowing my tears to flow.

## SOMATIC POP-UP

Sitting or lying down, use your left hand to gently squeeze your right arm, from your shoulder down to your fingertips. Repeat on your left arm, then move to your legs and use both hands to gently squeeze from your thighs down to your ankles. Take deep breaths as you squeeze, focusing on the sensation and pressure. Note how you feel. (Shifts focus to physical sensations, promoting a sense of calm and grounding.)

This sucks and right now I don't need to get my shit together.

I grieve for my hard-earned grief.

Right now, all I need to do is be gloomy.

## SOMATIC POP-UP

Seated or lying down, scan your body for an area where you feel sadness and gently place your hands there. Take a few easy breaths as you direct your attention to where your hands are in contact with your body. Lengthen your breath and visualize sending your exhale directly into that sad spot. With each exhale imagine the sad spot glows a little brighter until it's glowing like a hot coal. Then take one last big breath and exhale into the spot like a great cooling wind. (Activates the parasympathetic nervous system and enhances the mind-body connection.)

I feel sad.

Wipe your tears with this page. That's it. Dab your cheeks with the page or let your tears drip onto it. Let them stain the paper. Run your hand over the wet spots. Focus on your tears. Take a deep breath in and sigh, letting out a soft "huhhhh" sound. Note how it feels.

# Section 4: Hurt

## How Do You Do, Fellow Wounded Warrior

We have come to a very important section of this journal: hurt. In my work as a therapist, locating and honoring a client's core pain point is where I have witnessed their most powerful *Aha!* moments. These moments do not come right away or easily. Time must be spent untangling more easily accessible emotions, such as hostility, worry, or helplessness, before we can detect hurt. But most times, it is hurt that lies underneath our most powerful negative feelings. Hurt can show up as a doubt, question, or self-deprecative statement. *Could I be unlovable? Am I a bad person? This feeling is stupid. I am stupid.* Because these secret beliefs of inadequacy are so uncomfortable, we protect ourselves from them with defenses. That is why they are hard to locate, feel, and honor.

In this part of the journal, you get to revel in the very smallest part of yourself. Hurt likes to blame and project and justify and legitimize, but if we keep gently nudging defenses aside, we can get to hurt's soft underbelly, the pencil tip pain point, the root of our activation, triggers, and emotional turmoil. If we stay just a bit longer in hurt, we can begin to tolerate it just enough so that defenses don't take over. Little by little, we achieve affect tolerance, or the ability to have patience with pain. So, here the tender work of expressing your hurt begins. Engage with your hurt to recognize the delicate and beautiful nature of *you*.

Your hurt is welcome here.

Hurt happens and hurt has happened to me.

Nobody gets to define my shitty pain but me.

SOMATIC POP-UP

Sitting, interlace your fingers and place them in your lap. Send your attention to your hands holding each other. Send your inner focus into your clasped hands each time you exhale. Note how you feel. (Activates relaxation by engaging parasympathetic nervous system, directs focus toward tactile sensation and self-comfort.)

My wounds feel like crap, just the way they are supposed to feel.

The core of my being holds this hurt.

**SOMATIC POP-UP**

Sitting, place your palms on your thighs. Press gently and slide your palms up and down your thighs about ten times. Note how you feel. (Gentle self-massage relieves tension, activates blood circulation, and releases endorphins.)

I honor the pain that my humanness demands.

Damage has been done, and now I sit in the shit show.

### SOMATIC POP-UP

Sitting or standing, look straight ahead. See something and name it in your head. Turn your head to the right and look over your right shoulder, allowing your hips to open and rotate a little. See something behind you and name it in your head. Do the same for the left side. Note how you feel. (Vagus nerve stimulation triggers reset in the stress cycle.)

I validate my shit-induced brokenness before putting myself back together.

It is normal to feel shattered when something important to me is shat upon.

## SOMATIC POP-UP

Sitting or lying down, inhale and stretch your body out as long and wide as it can go. Exhale, contract your whole body by bringing your knees to your nose (or as close as you can get). Do this three times. Note how you feel. (Expanding and contracting movements replicate neurodevelopment patterns that help to strengthen the central nervous system.)

My heartache is not bullshit. It has a purpose.

I will not allow anyone to take a crap
on my honorable feelings of dejection.

## SOMATIC POP-UP

Sitting or standing, take your fingertips and lightly tap your temples, the bridge of your nose, and then your jaw. Let your fingertips gently pitter patter along those places and then the top of your head, like little rain drops. Note how you feel. (Stimulates acupressure points believed to influence the flow of energy in your body.)

Oh shit.

This

f\*cking

hurts.

I am in pain and it's gonna have to be OK for now.

### SOMATIC POP-UP

Sitting or standing, turn your pointer and middle fingers into a V, like scissors. Place your middle finger in front of your ear and your pointer finger behind your ear. Press down and run your fingers up and down in front and behind your ear and down the side of the jaw, giving yourself a gentle self-massage. Note how you feel. (Self-massage activates sense of agency in self-care.)

I need to be in the incomprehension of this shitty state of being.

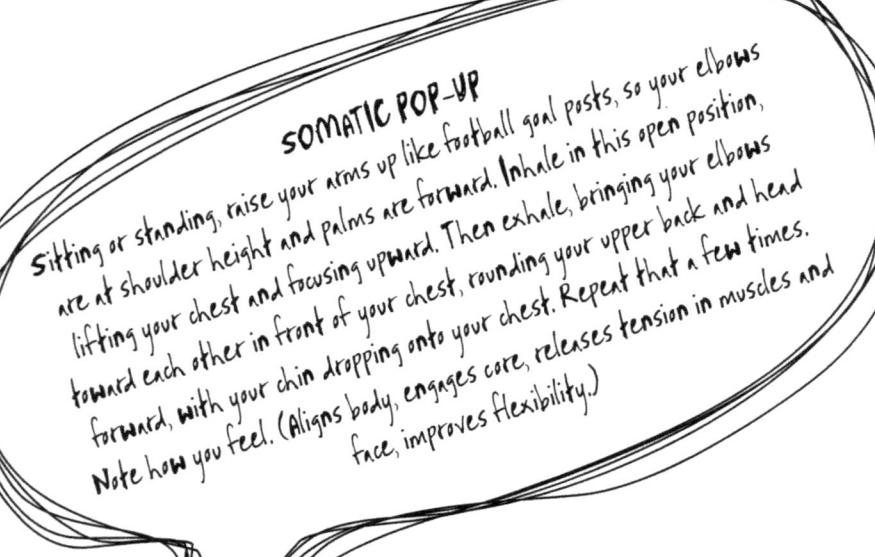

**SOMATIC POP-UP**

Sitting or standing, raise your arms up like football goal posts, so your elbows are at shoulder height and palms are forward. Inhale in this open position, lifting your chest and focusing upward. Then exhale, bringing your elbows toward each other in front of your chest, rounding your upper back and head forward, with your chin dropping onto your chest. Repeat that a few times. Note how you feel. (Aligns body, engages core, releases tension in muscles and face, improves flexibility.)

# Section 5: True Self

## Welcome Perfectly Imperfect You

You have landed at your destination: true self. After tracing your road of reactivity, you can now use this information to reframe how you interact with the world. Rather than negating or gratuitously affirming yourself away from harsh sensations, you have mindfully integrated them into your mind and body. True self is not perfection. It is not a "better self." True self means that you honor your complexity – your vulnerabilities and strengths – and how they are all connected. Consciously holding your emotional depth is the best thing you can ask of yourself. In true self, you navigate forward with sensorial and cognitive awareness - embodiment. This naturally alters the way you interact with people and your environment. Consciousness of self changes self. So, now you pay tribute to a new dynamic of selfhood. You are in a powerful state, full of potential and realness.

You, as you are, are welcome here.

I accept that I have shit to deal with.

I know my shit and I'm putting it to good use.

## SOMATIC POP-UP

Sitting or standing, breathe in and lift your arms above your head. As you exhale, make a quick sharp "sh" sounds while you flick your hands and wrists out as if you were shaking water off your fingertips. Shake and flick the imaginary water off as you slowly bring your arms down from above your head, down the sides of your body, all the way until your fingers point down toward the floor. Note how you feel. (The "sh" sound creates a physical sensation of calm while the wrist shaking reduces pressure on the median nerve.)

I may be messy, but I'm not full of shit.

My shit is a part of me, not all of me.

**SOMATIC POP-UP**

Sitting or standing, gently shake your left arm, then your right arm, then left leg and right leg. Wiggle, rock, and tip your pelvis, then slide your rib cage side to side, front and back. Lastly, tilt you head side to side and up and down. (Isolated movements increase blood flow to the brain. Awareness of body part functionality supports recognizing physical manifestations of stress.)

I am OK enough.

I have learned something new about myself and now I'm going to f\*cking rock it.

## SOMATIC POP-UP

Sit in a chair. Feel your booty in the seat of the chair. Feel your back against the back of the chair. Feel your feet on the floor. Notice the contact your body is making with anything that you are touching: your chair, clothes, jewelry, even the air. Note how you feel. (Attuning to the body's contact with the environment supports grounding in the present moment and tactile soothing.)

Being right where I need to be, right now, is The Shit.

## SOMATIC POP-UP

Seated or lying down, close your eyes and place the palms of your hands over your eyes, applying gentle pressure. Take deep, slow breaths into your belly, in through your nose and out through your mouth. Continue this for a few minutes, focusing on the sensation of your breath and the pressure on your eyes.

Note how you feel. (Activates the parasympathetic nervous system and shifts the nervous system into a safe, still state.)

I am not crap.

I am going do something really f*cking cool with this shit.

The story of me is still being written
and I'm a damn good biographer.

Perfection is not the objective.

I am dealing with my shit.

## SOMATIC POP-UP

Sitting, rest your hands on your thighs. Take a deep breath in and lift your chin while sliding your hips backward, creating an arch in your back. Pause in the arch at the top of your inhale, then on the exhale, move your head towards your chest and bring your tailbone forward, curving your spine. Note how you feel. (Releases emotions, enhances creativity and focus.)

I really give a shit about myself.

Holy shit, I am f*cking growing.

## SOMATIC POP-UP

Seated or lying down, scan your body for a place that holds peace. It can be any part of the body, small or large. Send your focus and breath there, paying attention to the qualities of that part of your body, like its shape, color, texture, or symbolic imagery. Slowly, with each breath, visualize the qualities of that part of your body emanating outward until your entire body is filled with the energy of the initial body part that felt peace. Note how you feel. (Identifies positive physical sensations or experiences within the body to promote safety, acting as an anchor for successful navigation of challenging situations.)

I feel my true self.

Close this book and lay it down next to you. Look up and as far out as you can. Lift your chest and drop your shoulders down and back. Take a big deep breath in, filling your chest and belly with air, and then slowly exhale out. You are here. Notice how it feels.

# Conclusion

*"I am out with lanterns, looking for myself."*
*~Emily Dickinson*

I'm not sure when or why it was decided that anger, fear, sadness, and hurt are negative emotions, because on the road to understanding true self, they can be positive indicators that guide us closer to our values and integrity. When we take the time to honestly explore our challenging emotions, we move away from repression and into the full complexity of our existence. I have sat in too many therapy sessions where clients try to convince themselves out of difficult feelings because they have been taught that they must fix, not feel; do, not be.

By working through the steps outlined in this journal, you have done something to resist the social norms that turn you against your feelings, instead letting them teach you. By traveling the road of reactivity, you have given yourself the gift of understanding how your activation is connected to your hurt, and you can now put that understanding to good use by keeping it in your consciousness as you interact with your loved ones and community. As you move forward from here, consider the following ways you might use your new insight for further reform.

- Show solidarity with others who are trying to change. Support those who work against the tyranny of repression.
- Share your feelings with others to resist norms that tell women to stay silent.
- Create goals and plans that move your life toward congruence with your true self.
- Respectfully resist those who dismiss women's valid thoughts and feelings.
- Be aware. Do not use your emotions to engage in the same oppression that you fight against.

Because you have traversed the path outlined within these pages, you now have clear markers on how to navigate life's crazy road ahead. You have expressed and moved your way through some tough shit. You have the tools for whatever comes your way!